BOYS R

# Race Car Dreamers

Felice Arena and Phil Kettle

illustrated by
Bettina Guthridge

RISING ★ STARS

First published in Great Britain by
RISING STARS UK LTD 2005
76 Farnaby Road, Bromley, BR1 4BH
Reprinted 2006

For information visit our website at:
www.risingstars-uk.com

British Library Cataloguing in Publication Data

A CIP record for this book is available from the British Library.

ISBN: 1-904591-98-1

First published in 2004 by
MACMILLAN EDUCATION AUSTRALIA PTY LTD
627 Chapel Street, South Yarra, Australia 3141

Visit our website at www.macmillan.com.au

Associated companies and representatives throughout the world.

Project Management by Limelight Press Pty Ltd
Cover and text design by Lore Foye
Illustrations by Bettina Guthridge

Printed in Malaysia

# Contents

CHAPTER 1
**The Idea**     **1**

CHAPTER 2
**Wheels and More**     **5**

CHAPTER 3
**Go-kart Builders**     **9**

CHAPTER 4
**Red Racing Machine**     **14**

CHAPTER 5
**Killer Hill**     **20**

EXTRA STUFF

- Racing Lingo     33
- Racing Must-dos     34
- Racing Instant Info     36
- Think Tank     38
- Hi Guys! (Author Letter)     40
- When We Were Kids     42
- What a Laugh!     43

*Josh*     *Con*

# CHAPTER 1

# The Idea

Josh and Con are sitting in an old car in Con's garage. The car is on a set of blocks—it has no wheels. The best friends talk about what it would be like to be racing car drivers.

**Con** "Imagine if we were old enough
to race. How cool would that be?"

**Josh** "Yes, it'd be unreal. Look
out Michael Schumacher, here
we come!"

**Con** "I wish it was ten years from
now and then we could race this."

**Josh** "Yes, but it'd be a bit hard in
a car that doesn't move."

**Con** "Maybe we could build our own racing car?"

**Josh** "What? Now? Cool."

**Con** "I reckon we've got enough stuff in the garage to build the best racing car in the world."

**Josh** "What are we going to use for a motor?"

**Con** "Maybe we could make a car without a motor and just race it down some hill?"

**Josh** "Yes, but it won't be a car exactly. Will it?"

**Con** "No, but it'll be the next best thing."

**Josh** "What?"

**Con** "A go-kart!"

CHAPTER 2

# **Wheels and More**

Con and Josh start to hunt through
the garage to find things that they
can use to build their go-kart. They
pile it all up in the middle of the
garage floor.

**Con** "Right, I think we've got
everything we need."

**Josh** "The only thing that we haven't got is ... "

**Con** "Is what?"

**Josh** "We haven't got any wheels."

**Con** "Yes, I know, we've got to get some."

**Josh** "Where from?"

Con thinks for a moment—his hands on his hips and face all screwed up.

**Josh** "I know where!"

**Con** "Where?"

**Josh** "From my sister's bike, she hardly ever uses it."

**Con** "Cool! But that's only two wheels. We still need to find another two."

The boys stand still and start to think again.

**Con** "Maybe … I could take the
wheels off my father's golf buggy?"

**Josh** "Brilliant idea! We could put
them back after we've finished
racing the cart."

**Con** "And we could put the wheels
back on your sister's bike, too."

**Josh** "It's a plan! I'll go and get my
sister's bike wheels and you get
the wheels from your father's
golf buggy."

# CHAPTER 3

# **Go-kart Builders**

Shortly after, the boys are walking back to the garage with the wheels.

**Con**  "Did your sister get upset when you told her that you were taking her bike wheels?"

**Josh** "No, she never said a word."

**Con** "You didn't ask her, did you?"

**Josh** "No! Did you ask your father whether you could borrow his golf buggy wheels?"

**Con** "Sort of."

**Josh** "What do you mean sort of?"

**Con** "Um, not really."

**Josh** "We'd better make sure that we put them back after we finish. They'll never know the difference."

The garage is soon filled with the sound of hammers banging and saws sawing.

**Con** "I can't wait for the day my dad lets me use all his electric tools."

**Josh** "Well, I hope that's a long way off. You're dangerous enough with a hammer and an ordinary saw."

**Con** "Dad reckons that by the time
he lets me use his proper tools
I'll be so old that I won't be able
to lift them."

Soon the boys have nailed more
wood to the plank to make a seat.
They have also managed to attach
axles and wheels to the plank.

**Con**  "All we need to do now is tie some rope to the front axle so we can steer, and our racing cart is ready to roll."

**Josh** (grinning)  "You mean our *Formula One racing car*!"

## CHAPTER 4

# Red Racing Machine

The boys catch sight of some paint cans on the shelves in the garage.

**Con** "I think we should borrow some of Dad's red paint. The cart will go a lot faster if it's painted red."

**Josh** "Yes, red's a cool racing colour!"

The boys take the tin of red paint and paint the go-kart. They manage to get as much paint on the garage floor as on the cart.

**Josh**  "It looks so cool."

**Con**  "Yes, totally hot. Now it's ready to rumble!"

**Josh** "So where are we going to race it?"

**Con** "What about 'Killer Hill'?"

**Josh** "Yeah—but we're going to have to get a heap of safety gear first. That hill has messed up a lot of skateboarders and bike riders before."

Con and Josh leave the garage, and moments later return wearing safety gear.

**Con** "You've got so much on, you look like you've just come from an outer-space flight."

**Josh** "Well, you totally need it when you're a professional car racer, you know."

Both boys have their bike helmets
on. Con has pillows taped to his legs
and his father's leather jacket on.

**Josh** "Your dad's old biker jacket
looks really cool."
**Con** "Thanks, but I'm not so sure
about those on you."

**Josh** "They're Mum's cleaning gloves. They're much better than any racing gloves I've ever seen."

**Con** "Well, let's go then! Killer Hill, here we come!"

# CHAPTER 5

# Killer Hill

Con and Josh tow their go-kart to
Killer Hill—a grassy hill located in a
park at the end of their street.

**Con** "Gee, it's a lot steeper than you
think when you get to the top and
look down."

**Josh** "Yes, lucky we've got all this safety gear on."

**Con** "But I've just remembered what we forgot."

**Josh** "What?"

**Con** "Brakes!"

**Josh** "It doesn't matter. It'll roll to a stop by itself when we get to the bottom."

**Con** "I hope so."

**Josh** "You scared? Because *real* racing car drivers love fear, you know!"

**Con** "Yes, you're right. And we're the best racing car drivers around—well, in this park, anyway. Let's do it!"

Con and Josh point the go-kart towards the bottom of the hill.

**Con** "Okay, this is it."
**Josh** "Who's going to sit at the front?"

The boys look at each other.

**Con and Josh** "You!!!"
**Con** "I think you should. You're the oldest."

**Josh** "Yes, but only by two weeks.
Okay then, I'll do it. Ready? GO!!!"

The boys push the go-kart off with
their feet, and quickly jump in.
Within seconds the cart is zooming
down the hill.

**Con and Josh**

"AAAARRRGHHHH!!!!!!!!!!!!"

**Josh** (shouting)  "It's really hard to steer!"

**Con** (shouting)  "We're going to die!"

**Con and Josh**

"AAAARRRGHHHH!!!!!!!!!!!!"

Suddenly the boys realise that they
are heading directly for Con's dog
who has wandered in front of them.

**Josh** (shouting)  "Oh no! We're
heading straight for him!"

**Con** (shouting) "Look out! Josh! Josh! Turn! Turn!"

**Josh** (shouting) "I'm trying!"

**Con** (shouting) "He hasn't seen us. We're going to run over him."

**Con and Josh**

"AAAARRRGHHHH!!!!!!!!!!!!"

Just in time Josh steers the cart
past the dog and on down the hill.

**Con** "That was close."
**Josh** "Lucky I'm a good dri—"
**Con** (shouting) "Look out for the—"

*Smash!* Josh and Con crash into
a tree.

**Josh** "You okay?"

**Con** "Yes. You?"

**Josh** "Yes. It was unreal, we were flying. Now I know what racing car drivers mean when they say they have 'the need for speed'."

**Josh** "Wow! We have the need for speed."

**Con** "Hey! Let's do it again."

The boys hop out of the go-kart and drag it back to the top of Killer Hill. Seconds later, they're speeding down it once again, this time with Con in the front, steering.

**Con** "AAAARRRGHHHH!!!!!!!!!!! It's worse up front than I thought."

**Josh** "Don't freak out. Just steer it straight. Look out for that bump!"

But it's too late, and Josh, Con and the go-kart fly into the air and then land with an almighty thud—the two front wheels snapping off completely.

**Con** "I don't think I have the need for speed anymore."

**Josh** "Yes, I was thinking the same thing!"

**Con** "But I do have the need
for food."

**Josh** "You must be a mind reader.
That's what I was thinking, too."

The boys pick themselves up,
collect the two front wheels and start
towards home. They decide they've
had enough of race car dreaming—at
least for today.

# Racing Lingo

*Josh*  *Con*

**brakes** They lock up the wheels of a car to help it to stop.

**burnout** When the tyres spin on the road and smoke comes from them.

**petrol head** A person who really loves car racing.

**prang** When you crash your car.

**pro go-kart** Like your go-kart, but with a motor for racing.

**spin-out** When you lose control of the car that you are driving.

# BOYS RULE!

# Racing Must-dos

☞ Always make sure that you wear a helmet.

☞ Wear really cool-looking sunglasses.

☞ Learn to like lots of loud noise.

☞ Paint your go-kart red. Red is a really fast colour.

☞ Wear driving gloves. They may not help you go faster, but they help you look really cool!

☞ Check the steering before you take off. While you're at it, check your wheels too—make sure they're attached securely.

☞ Make sure that you have plenty of pillows to sit on.

☞ Try to go as fast as you can.

☞ Paint the number "1" on your cart.

☞ Avoid driving into trees. It's not good for your go-kart—or you.

☞ Have some practice runs down some small hills before tackling the bigger ones.

# BOYS RULE!

# Racing Instant Info

A black and white chequered flag is waved to the drivers at the end of a race.

If you happen to get the chequered flag waved at you, that means you have won the race!

A Formula One racing car can travel at a speed of 360 kilometres per hour.

"Days of Thunder" was a hit movie made in the 1980s starring Tom Cruise. It was about racing cars.

The first go-kart races took place in California, USA in 1956.

Most go-karts are about 1.5 metres in length.

Most go-karts are usually open, with railings for bumpers.

The town of Bangalow in NSW, Australia, stages a go-kart derby every year.

To build your own go-kart you'll need at least 3 metres of timber— and 4 wheels of course!

# Think Tank

1 Do motors need fuel to make them work?

2 What does it mean if you get the chequered flag waved at you?

3 What is a burnout?

4 How many wheels are there on a go-kart?

5 Should you wear a helmet when you drive a go-kart?

6 Why do drivers wear sunglasses?

7 If you see a stop sign, what do you have to do?

8 Do you think that you could build a go-kart?

# Answers

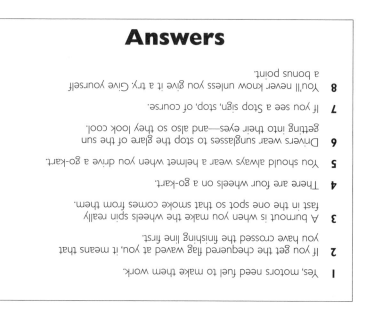

**1** Yes, motors need fuel to make them work.

**2** If you get the chequered flag waved at you, it means that you have crossed the finishing line first.

**3** A burnout is when you make the wheels spin really fast in the one spot so that smoke comes from them.

**4** There are four wheels on a go-kart.

**5** You should always wear a helmet when you drive a go-kart.

**6** Drivers wear sunglasses to stop the glare of the sun getting into their eyes—and also so they look cool.

**7** If you see a Stop sign, stop, of course.

**8** You'll never know unless you give it a try. Give yourself a bonus point.

# How did you score?

- If you got all 8 answers correct, you're ready for your first go-kart race.

- If you got 6 answers correct, then you're ready for a go-kart race, but only as a co-driver.

- If you got fewer than 4 answers correct, then watch a few go-kart races first before you try it.

Felice → ← Phil

## Hi Guys!

We have heaps of fun reading and want you to, too. We both believe that being a good reader is really important and so cool.

Try out our suggestions to help you have fun as you read.

At school, why don't you use "Race Car Dreamers" as a play and you and your friends can be the actors. Set the scene for your play. Bring your bike helmet and safety gear to school to use as props and use your acting skills and imagination to pretend that you are taking part in an important Formula One racing car event.

So ... have you decided who is going to be Con and who is going to be Josh? Now, with your friends, read and act out our story in front of the class.

We have a lot of fun when we go to schools and read our stories. After we finish the kids all clap really loudly. When you've finished your play your classmates will do the same. Just remember to look out the window—there might be a talent scout from a television station watching you!

Reading at home is really important and a lot of fun as well.

Take our books home and get someone in your family to read them with you. Maybe they can take on a part in the story.

Remember, reading is a whole lot of fun.

So, as the frog in the local pond would say, Read-it!

And remember, Boys Rule!

**Phil** "Did you ever think you could've been a good racing car driver?"

**Felice** "I thought I'd have been the best! What about you?"

**Phil** "I know I would have. I learnt to drive when I was really young."

**Felice** "How come?"

**Phil** "I lived on a farm and my father taught me to drive a tractor when I was only eight."

**Felice** "Did you have any accidents?"

**Phil** "One day I ran over a fence post."

**Felice** "Maybe you should've considered being a crash-and-smash driver instead."

# BOYS RULE!
# What a Laugh!

**Q** What happens when a frog's car breaks down?

**A** It gets toad away.

# BOYS RULE!

| | | | | |
|---|---|---|---|---|
| Gone Fishing | The Tree House | Golf Legends | Camping Out | Bike Daredevils |
| Water Rats | Skateboard Dudes | Tennis Ace | Basketball Buddies | Secret Agent Heroes |
| Wet World | Rock Star | Pirate Attack | Olympic Champions | Race Car Dreamers |
| Hit the Beach | Rotten School Day | Halloween Gotcha! | Battle of the Games | On the Farm |